Animales del zoológico / Zoo Animals

LOS MONOS
MONKEYS
AT THE ZOO

Seth Lynch

Traducido por / Translated by Esther Ortiz

Gareth Stevens
PUBLISHING

Please visit our website, www.garethstevens.com. For a free color catalog of all our high-quality books, call toll free 1-800-542-2595 or fax 1-877-542-2596.

Library of Congress Cataloging-in-Publication Data

Names: Lynch, Seth, author.
Title: Los monos / Monkeys at the zoo / Seth Lynch.
Description: New York : Gareth Stevens Publishing, [2020] | Series: Animales del zoológico / Zoo animals | Includes index.
Identifiers: LCCN 2018039584| ISBN 9781538243596 (library bound)
Subjects: LCSH: Monkeys–Juvenile literature. | Zoo animals–Juvenile literature.
Classification: LCC QL737.P9 L95 2020 | DDC 599.8–dc23
LC record available at https://lccn.loc.gov/2018039584

First Edition

Published in 2020 by
Gareth Stevens Publishing
111 East 14th Street, Suite 349
New York, NY 10003

Translator: Esther Ortiz
Editor, English: Therese Shea
Designer: Katelyn E. Reynolds

Photo credits: Cover, p. 1 vblinov/Shutterstock.com; p. 5 FamVeld/Shutterstock.com; p. 7 Don Mammoser/Shutterstock.com; pp. 9, 24 (tail) ChameleonsEye/Shutterstock.com; p. 11 Julia Moiseenko/Shutterstock.com; p. 13 Iakov Filimonov/Shutterstock.com; p. 15 Henk Bogaard/Shutterstock.com; pp. 17, 24 (mandrill) SawBear/Shutterstock.com; pp. 19, 24 (troop) Nick Fox/Shutterstock.com; p. 21 Ryan M. Bolton/Shutterstock.com; p. 23 Evikka/Shutterstock.com.

Printed in the United States of America

CPSIA compliance information: Batch #CS19GS: For further information contact Gareth Stevens, New York, New York at 1-800-542-2595.

Contenido

Aprendamos sobre los monos 4
La cola de los monos 8
Tipos de monos 12
Una manada de monos 18
Inteligentes y divertidos. 20
Palabras que debes aprender. 24
Índice 24

Contents

Learning About Monkeys 4
Monkey Tails 8
Kinds of Monkeys. 12
Monkey Troop 18
Smart and Funny! 20
Words to Know 24
Index. 24

Veo monos
en el zoológico.
¡Aprendo mucho!

....

I see monkeys
at the zoo.
I learn a lot!

La mayoría de monos
vive en los árboles.

Most monkeys
live in trees.

Los monos tienen cola.

Monkeys have tails.

Algunas colas
son pequeñas.

Some tails are small.

¡Hay más de 200 tipos de monos!

There are more than 200 kinds of monkeys!

Los babuinos son
un tipo de monos.
Viven en el suelo.

Baboons are monkeys.
They live on the ground.

El mono más grande
es el mandril.

The largest monkey
is the mandrill.

Un grupo de monos
es una manada.

A group of monkeys
is a troop.

Los monos son inteligentes.
¡También son divertidos!

Monkeys are smart.
Monkeys are funny!

Me gustan los monos
del zoológico.

....

I like the monkeys
at the zoo!

Palabras que debes aprender
Words to Know

(el) mandril
mandrill

(la) cola
tail

(la) manada
troop

Índice/Index

babuinos / baboons 14

cola / tail 8, 10

manada / troop 18

mandril / mandrill 16